WISDOM OF THE WILD ONES

A SPIRITUAL NARRATIVE

FARNAZ N. RENEKER

KRISTIN WHITE

ACKNOWLEDGMENTS

Farnaz:
To Mother Earth for showing me the beauty of life in all forms on the planet.
To my Earth mother for her continuous support, friendship, and sharing the gifts of alchemy from our ancestors.
To my Galactic mothers for their teachings, understanding, and unconditional love.
As above, so below. As within, so without.

———

Kristin:
For the furry creatures with whom I have shared this lifetime. You have entertained me, broken my heart, and soothed my soul unlike any human.
I hope when I leave this Earth, you will all come running to greet me and I can gather you in my arms and put my nose in all your fur at the same time.

———

CONTENTS

PREFACE

NOTE FROM THE AUTHORS

Farnaz:

Kristin and I channeled the content for our first collaborative text in 2020, a year of great transformation. We were honored to receive the information and share it in *The Love Frequency: A Guide to Oneness,* published in May of 2021. For readers unfamiliar with the contents, the key messages that flowed through us from a greater universal source focused on the power of the human heart and the ripple effect of unconditional love.

In 2021, a year of expansion, we began channeling the contents of the following text. Completely unusual and truly wild were our inter-dimensional encounters with the consciousness of wild animals and spirits of the natural world. The messages contained within *Wisdom of the Wild Ones* delivers an unexpected perspective of our place within the tapestry of this planet we call home.

I encourage you to feel into the energies, rather than purely the words, emanating from the wild ones — there is, indeed, wisdom within.

Kristin:

After our first book, *The Love Frequency*, was published, my spiritual beliefs were suddenly out there for the world to know. No longer held tight within, I felt freer to talk about the incredible spiritual and natural events that I had been experiencing that seemed otherworldly and magnificent, yet I also felt nervous about the judgment that I feared existed among people, including good friends, who do not see the world similarly.

As I prepared for tough conversations, I was shocked that they never happened. I found that many friends, whom I expected to either ignore the book or challenge my experiences, were actually curious, shared their own stories, and asked the most interesting questions.

I learned about a team of angels who spoke directly to a friend and held her during a devastating miscarriage.

I learned that my rocket scientist friend, whom I really expected to give me the side eye, was opening up to unexplainable energies she was experiencing during Reiki and meditation sessions.

I learned that strangers wanted to hold my hand and touch my face and come experience my sound bath sessions.

I learned to let my light shine without fear of judgment and that I don't have to be a guru to add a little understanding to this world we share.

Enjoy *Wisdom of the Wild Ones*. It's a wild one!

NOTE TO THE READER

All channeled messages are noted as such in the chapter subtitles and unaltered from the original transmissions. Clarifications from the authors are noted in brackets [...] and channeled questions are *italicized*.

Through the vocal channeling process, there are often pauses within the transmission, which are noted in the type with dashes (--).

As you read the channeled text, you may consider pausing often, as it is in the space in between words that we receive the depth of the transmissions.

INTRODUCTION: THE CATS
BY AGATHA NOBLE

Domesticated felines date back some 10,000 years ago. Wild cats were drawn to agricultural development as rodents were centralized in these zones. As hunters, the cats were respected as they saved concentrated populations from disease, food shortage, and destruction. In Egypt, cats were revered animals, and Cleopatra was the "mother cat," a symbol of power and fertility. On the tombs of Thebes, where the pharaohs are buried, an inscription reads: "Thou art the Great Cat, the avenger of gods, and the judge of worlds, and the president of the sovereign chiefs and the governor of the holy Circle; thou art indeed the Great Cat." *Leo*, the mythological lion, was deemed untouchable by men. The constellation became the inspiration behind the Sphinx – the half-lion, half-man who inspired the annual flooding of the Nile – a critical part of a successful harvest.

In Russian folklore, Baun was known as a cunning and magical cat – capable of healing any illness. Though Baun was *capable,* he was known to keep his powers to himself. In fact, those who tried to seek out the mystical cat were often lulled to sleep and eaten. In China, the *senri* (or *nekata* in Japan) were old leopards that transformed into men. Like demons, they stole the souls of humans, then fully inhabited their transfigured bodies.

In Puritan America, cats were known as companions to witches. Throughout the early centuries of the nation, cats were hanged and buried because it was believed that witches could shape shift into cats on a full moon. Men laid blessed salt on witches' houses to protect the town from evil.

Why were cats contrastingly revered or demonized in history? Why are they anthropomorphized and misunderstood? Why were they once viewed as malevolent predators and evil shapeshifters? Like many things in human history, events and characters who were not understood were maligned to darkness. Today, though "evil spirits" do not dominate the consciousness of the western hemisphere, fear does. The thread that connects Russian folklore to Chinese myth: fear. The reality behind the Egyptians' reverence: fear. They feared that without reverence the gods would blight their crops. Reverence, thus, meant survival.

"EVEN IN MODERNITY WE HEAR OF THE CAGED CAT — CONFINED FOR OUR PLEASURE, OUR AMUSEMENT." — RAINER MARIA RILKE: "THE PANTHER."

Though fear plays a critical role in humans' evolutionary development, especially in the pre-tribal landscape without weapons or adequate shelter, we now live, mostly, without primal fear. The human narrative has changed. And yet, our brains remain wired to an ancient one. It is my earnest and fervent belief that Kristin and Farnaz are *changing* the narrative and beginning the process of re-wiring humanity. Let me explain.

It is important to note that the previous tales are of mostly domesticated cats, but like all mammal taxonomies, there is a particular genetic thread that runs from the house bred felines to the wild ones. The *panthera*, the *neofelis*, the *acinonyx*, and the *puma* reside under the house of *Felidae*. These are majestic and magical creatures that live beyond the boundaries and edges of "our" world. Their homesteads are not traced with salt, columns, tombs, or containment, but blooming with wild vines, bulging roots, and thick forests. Additionally, they cannot be pinned down by myth, but are beholden only to an 11.5-million-year-old ancestry. In other words, they are earthly gods.

These animals are also not confined by the limits of *our* imagination; they are transcendent and unruly. They are Mothers; they are daring; they speak to us *as* our ancestors. From transcendent places within our hearts and from the farthest reaches of the universe's dimensions that we have yet to comprehend, the Cats speak to the authors of this book with clarity and hope. What we do know of these ancestral, ancient beings is the language of love, the language of possibility. Like the sphinx, Farnaz narrates a feline possession that offers hope. I cannot begin to define – let alone explain – the wild ones who speak. I do know, however, that our guides offer narratives of compassion. We only have to be held by the wild ones. We can let them hold our hearts as we now understand that these big cats are neither predatory nor are they governed by human understanding. Farnaz and Kristin are aware of this, which can make the stepping *into* the text challenging. My request is that as you are held by the words, the prayer, the invocation, that you let go the limits of your imagination. Let the words flow. Let them move over you. Our evolution is coming.

1

INTO THE WILDERNESS

Farnaz:

Boldness. Courage.

Both are needed when we leap into the vast unknown.

There are no guarantees of where we will land upon jumping.

There are no roadmaps for our wildest adventures.

There is no discovery without risk.

The lion within me is bold and courageous.

She is fearless because she trusts her innate knowing that life is to be lived without certainty.

She reminds me that within the uncertainty lies the magic and as long as I live from my heart, the universe will always support me.

2

———

SIGNS & SYMBOLS

INTRODUCTION

Farnaz:

We are all born into this lifetime with immense wisdom in our cells and a remembering of who we are at the core. We sense a deep knowing of all the intricate ways we are interconnected with all that is. Sometimes we forget – go to sleep – for long periods of time, even decades. But, once we wake up, we witness the magic of our interconnection in ways that both shock and delight us.

Kristin and I began our journey with the wild ones in January 2021. It was a Sunday morning when we came together, after a few days of preparation – body, mind, and spirit. We laid out a ceremonial spread, or altar, between us as we remained seated on meditation cushions in the special room of her home.

At the center of the purple fabric, we placed a spherical sunset iolite crystal, which had been uniquely coded for me by a gifted medium to assist in a deeper connection with the love frequency. Surrounding the crystal were other sacred objects, each with their own unique frequencies.

The channeling sessions that Kristin and I had grown accustomed to always began with a connection to the pure energy of the heart. As we closed our eyes and began breathing deeply to connect to the love frequency, I called in the energy of number nine – representing completion. We sensed the energies of several guides that were present.

In front of Kristin was a yellow-white energy to guide the questions to be asked. Behind me was the energy of a woman with short, black hair, wearing leopard print clothing. In her right hand, she held a spear – with a nod, she signaled to me that she would be my protector during the session.

I took another deep breath as an enormous orb encompassed us in a field of blue light – impressing it with a sense of trust, freedom, and love. In my mind's eye, I witnessed a powerful figure emerging from inside the spherical crystal at the center of the altar – a large, spotted wild cat. I began to describe my vision to Kristin.

--

Farnaz:

This energy is powerful, strong, grounding, fierce. I see a leopard or jaguar.

There is a seriousness in the leopard's eyes, yet still a very feminine type of energy – it reminds me of the energy between a mother and her child – stern yet loving.

The leopard is focused on me with her eyes. She says that her focused gaze is intended to show us how to be strong and grounded, yet soft and allowing – in the way that a mother raises her cubs.

She says that everything must be done with unconditional love.

She says the leopard beings are an advocate for the divine feminine, expressed as the fierceness of a mother's love for her children.

Similar to the way that a mother would only hurt another animal out of necessity to protect her own children – she is otherwise gentle and loving.

--

Then, the questions began flowing through Kristin, as the energy of the leopard's answers flowed through me.

3

SIGNS & SYMBOLS

CHANNELED MESSAGE: LEOPARDS

--

I see visions of a star, like a Merkabah star. Does this having meaning to you?

--

The Merkabah star is related to the Akashic records and the vehicle that your souls and bodies use to travel between planes of existence. When you travel from the Earth plane to other [etheric] planes, this sacred geometric form is the vehicle that envelops you and allows you to go to these different planes.

It protects you. It is you. It is an aspect of you.

Within the Merkabah are the memories of all of your soul's experiences, whether on the Earth plane or in other places in the universe. It contains the records of all that you have ever done or will do and have been or will be – because there is no linear time.

All the possibilities of you are contained in this star. You may tap into any aspect of yourself at any time and your cells will recognize or remember the memories of those experiences and draw them into your current experience as knowledge or wisdom.

--

I see beads, what can you tell us about strings of beads?

--

Each bead symbolizes one of your lifetimes. And although the beads occur in a specific order, one after the other, the string of beads forms a loop, or a circle. This is one way that we can explain to you the nonlinearity of your existence.

Depending on how this string of beads is placed on the palm of your hand – and you can try this several different ways – you will never perceive the string as a straight line. It will curve and bend and loop around.

As a single bead, you are not aware of the other beads, the string, or the fact that you are part of a whole. If the single bead represents your life now, and you are not aware of your connection to other lifetimes, then you perceive yourself in this life as a single lonely bead. But, in truth, there are infinite experiences that link to one another by the string.

The string is your core essence, or your Higher Self, which is the awareness that weaves through each and every lifetime. So, although each lifetime seems to be disconnected from the others, the Higher Self knows that they are all part of the same whole.

This is an analogy, so that you may be able to understand the depth of your connection to your Higher Self and so that you may begin to explore other facets of yourself. In this exploration, you may gain cellular memory from those other experiences. Perhaps the wisdom you gained from those experiences would benefit you in this lifetime, so that you do not need to repeat the same lessons.

--

Now I am seeing three symbols together. A crescent moon, a heart, and a diamond (like a gemstone).

--

The moon symbolizes feminine energies and the energy of turning inward.

The heart symbolizes the love frequency – the love of Creative Source energy within each human being.

We are showing you the diamond, or gemstone, to represent several things. The first is to represent the multi-faceted nature of each and every one of you. The second is to remind you to stay in your heart center and to go inward to reflect – until you have polished every facet of the gemstone that you are.

--

And now I see a four-leaf clover.

--

I think you know what this symbolizes [as the leopard laughs].

The four-leaf clover symbolizes, in addition to blessings or good fortune, a connection to nature.

A connection to nature is essential for the well-being of any human being, in terms of spending time in nature and becoming one with nature. We are also referring to the reverence and honoring of all divinity within nature – for the planet itself and for all life on the planet.

Also essential for your well-being is gratitude for these energies that sustain you and bring you joy. And the supportive energies of all of nature's spirits, who are here to serve you. Take time to give thanks for the blessings and supportive energies.

You have another question.

--

Yes.

Can you tell us more about nature's spirits and how we can communicate with them and recognize them?

--

All elements in nature have their own energies. They have their collective energies and their individual expressions. But they are all part of one: the Oneness. They are all manifestations of Creative Source energy.

In the same way that each human being has a purpose, each of nature's spirits has its own purpose. For example, there are many spirits in the ocean, but different groups have different roles. There is a group whose role is to help balance the oceans' waters throughout the planet – that is their purpose. There are tree spirits. There are flower spirits. Mineral spirits, which you call crystals.

Every piece of Source's creation has its own frequency and there is a purpose for that frequency.

As for getting to know them, unless you were born with the gift where you innately do, the only way is to set the intention and to take the time to commune with them.

So, if you take a flower, and you hold the petals in the palms of your hands, you appreciate the beauty in it, you softly gaze at it in reverence, the frequencies of the flower will be felt in your heart. And if you spend enough time with the flower and you practice this, the flower will communicate with you. Not necessarily in words, but in thought forms or as feelings. And you will get to know the spirit of the flower.

If you sit in the darkness, under the moonlight, and you gaze at the moon with reverence and love in your heart, the moon will speak to you.

This is a simple act, but it requires focus, going inward and feeling with your own heart frequency.

This was the way of the ancients that has been lost over time. You are being asked to bring these teachings back, so that regardless of age, every human being's experience is full of magic.

We will call it a benevolent magic, as this type of magic's only aim is to increase love on the planet between you and other humans, between you and animals, between you and all of nature.

And the way of the Shamans has always been to connect with and honor nature and to look to it for signs in order to answer human questions.

--

I see spirals, like a snail shell and Fibonacci patterns in nature, like pinecones.

--

These patterns of sacred geometry represent the infinite. They also represent the fractals that exist throughout the universe in all of Creative Source energy's manifestations.

You may choose to study fractals further. But how quickly you integrate your own personal understanding of fractals and the infinite will vary from person to person.

These spirals are visible in all aspects of nature as a reminder of the truth. And as a tool of study, for those who are interested.

--

I see crowns, like the kinds of spiky crowns that you see in Renaissance paintings and spiritual art.

--

These crowns are similar to the tops of buildings in Gothic architecture, are they not?

--

Yes.

--

Humans have always had an innate sense of the truth and attempted to express it in different forms.

The crown, whether expressed as a piece of jewelry to be placed on the head or the spire of a cathedral, symbolizes ascension, or movement upwards towards the light.

The crown represents a path to reaching higher levels of consciousness.

--

I see fish.

--

Fish are a primitive symbol of the source of Earth energies and well-being – fertility and abundance. They also represent spiritual freedom, as they flow with ease through the water. Their bodies are flexible, so they are able to bend and move fast or slow – a representation water energy.

--

When you see a symbol, whether it's with your open eyes or in your mind's eye, take a moment and reflect on what the symbol means to you. And the answers will come.

You all have the ability to do this. Some need more practice than others. The idea is to go with your first instinct, not thought. You want for this flow to be within your heart.

This is why we showed you the moon and heart symbols at the beginning of the session. Again, the moon represents going inward and the heart represents staying in your heart center.

This is the only way to strengthen your intuition, gain insight, and become the brilliant light bodies that you already are. And to polish the facets of the gem that you already are.

We are finished for today.

--

4

SIGNS & SYMBOLS

REFLECTION

Kristin:

As the energy tells us, the leopards are the guardians of the Divine Feminine and once I processed that information, their fierce nature made sense. If you read our first book, you might recall my description of the Divine Feminine energy as the softest, most gentle energy. It felt like a bath of pure, all-encompassing love around me. It was an energy that made me so peaceful and relaxed that I could barely form questions. So, when you think about the Divine Feminine, and what it would take to protect that soft, trusting energy, it only makes sense that it is protected by something quite fierce and strong.

Through our editor, Aggie, Farnaz and I were introduced to an extraordinary woman, Cheech, who left her medical practice to be with the big, wild cats in Africa. Cheech explained to us that the big cats were guided by instinct and instinct alone. They are not there to bond with humans and to make us feel loved or needed or even considered. If they stop to give us their time, they are guarded and no-nonsense in their interactions, and they communicate via "snapshots of signs and symbols," rather than through linear conversation.

I listened to her expert descriptions with my mouth agape. She precisely described my experience with the leopard energies. They were simply there to answer my questions, which came in the form of signs and symbols, and move on to the next task.

During the subsequent channels with them, I better understood my role and was grateful for the leopards' wisdom and respectful of their ferocity. Rather than feeling intimidated by them, I felt reverence.

5

———

DIVINE BALANCE

INTRODUCTION

K ristin:

Our experience with channeling has evolved since we first started. In the beginning, we were both excited, but a bit uneasy. Not knowing whether it would work, and a little nervous that something might break the magic, we would channel in the dark of night, when everything felt a bit more mysterious, as though that stacked the odds of success in our favor. But it always worked, so as time went on, we were less nervous, less formal, and gave over to the flow of it all.

Farnaz is the real star of the show. Her ability to fully embody and bring life and words to these energies is a sight to behold. I feel like I'm inside of a living, breathing miracle when I witness her channelling.

My role, to amplify and support the experience, is one I'm very comfortable in. I've done this in many different contexts throughout my life. I hold space for Farnaz and the energies, beam love into the experience, guide the experience through questions, and keep an eye out for our safety. It's a role of duality where I'm both in the experience and outside of the experience at the same time. Farnaz is deeper in, as she must be, in order to bring the energies into a form that we can understand. Similarly, to when I'm facilitating a sound bath, I must straddle two worlds so that I can protect and manage our surroundings, so that Farnaz feels safe enough to go deep.

On the day of the following channeling, we met in my meditation room on an average weekday morning. The kids were in school and the husbands at work, which was a nice set up for a focused channeling experience.

Our main guide for this session was a Hawaiian Kahuna – a wise man, or a Shaman. His masculine presence was needed for the channel with the feminine energies of the leopards to be in divine balance.

After inviting these energies to join us, we were guided to clear and balance each layer of our energetic bodies, one by one, through mindful breathing.

For each layer of the energy body, or aura, we commanded with love and appreciation for it to be balanced to divine perfection. After completing this cycle thirteen times, we took three deep breaths.

Farnaz then invited the energy of the number six, representing balance, and the majestic leopard energy emerged like a mist out of the crystal at the center of our altar.

Farnaz let me know she was ready for questions and suddenly I heard and felt bells ringing joyfully all around me.

From there the channeling continued for a while without interruptions, until my baby kitten, Sasquatch, made his presence known outside of the meditation room door. Between the two worlds, I was aware of Sassy's meows, but I assumed he would give up after some time and find excitement elsewhere. Farnaz continued channeling and was deep into explanation and talking very rapidly and excitedly as Sassy's' meows became more and more insistent. The more amplified Farnaz became, the louder Sassy became until finally I got up from the floor and opened the door. Without skipping a beat, Sassy lay in Farnaz's lap, curled up and went to sleep, leaving very loud purring noises on the sound recorder we use to tape the sessions.

Sasquatch is no ordinary kitten. He has a polydactyl genetic mutation giving him five extra toes, which makes him extra adorable. Polydactyls were considered witches' cats in Europe during the time of the Inquisition and the Dark Ages, which led to them being hunted and killed. I'm pretty sure he carries some of the magic of his ancestors. He is a baby, but he is also a wild one.

6

DIVINE BALANCE

CHANNELED MESSAGE: LEOPARDS

--

I hear and see a lot of bells ringing very joyfully. Can you give us some guidance around these bells?

--

Celebration is coming.

It is time for the divine feminine and divine masculine to come into perfect balance and harmony.

Humanity has waited a long time for this.

The bells are a signal that this [time] is coming – it will be a time of joy and celebration.

There will be no more wars or extreme conflict as the feminine energy is a uniter and acts compassionately. A mother would never send her children to war. The Earth will be led by the balanced energies of masculine and feminine.

--

I see the color violet, very vibrant and glowing and flowing. Can you tell us about the violet energy and how it relates to this time in our lives?

--

The violet ray is representative of transformation and transmutation. This relates to the energies which are currently being transformed to be in divine balance.

You can call in this color as you meditate for the well-being of the planet.

You can also call in this color when you are working through aspects of your lives that require transmutation [changing from one form to another].

Violet is the color associated with benevolent magic. It is also associated with the violet flame of [ascended master] St. Germaine.

--

I see a rock shooting up from the Earth, a very pointed, narrow, and tall pyramid. Are there messages around this?

--

The minerals, rocks, and crystals of the Earth hold memories of the events that took place in those specific areas.

Do you want to ask more questions about this?

--

It feels like something that is going to emerge at a certain time.

--

There are several messages around this.

One is that there is memory in the Earth, within the crystal caves inside of the Earth and within the crystalline energetic grid of the Earth.

The crystalline grid that surrounds and goes within the Earth is energetic and holds memories. There are memories of the events that took place there. There are memories around the frequencies of those events. And those frequencies are currently shifting. That's the first message.

The second is that these pyramids represent the sacred structures that were built in the Southern Hemisphere. For example, in Egypt or in Mexico, or at Machu Pichu.

The feminine energies in the Southern Hemisphere are rising to bring the masculine energies of the Northern Hemisphere into balance.

In a way, the third representation of this vision is the rising of the feminine energies to bring the Earth into divine balance. Or to bring the energies of the population of the Earth into divine balance.

--

What role do humans have to help make this happen?

Many of you are already doing this and it does not require all of humanity to be illuminated or enlightened by this information.

There are enough humans at this moment that are awakening; this is enough for the collective consciousness to shift in this direction.

What you may do in your personal daily lives is to stay in allowance. Go with the flow. And be as you are. So that your own divine feminine energy is in balance with your divine masculine energy.

--

Yes, thank you.

I see bright shiny stars that feels similar to the bells. Are there messages around the stars? Yellow, shiny bright stars in clusters.

--

Your helpers from other planets and galaxies are watching over you. And they are assisting with this rebalancing of energies on the planet. They are proud. They are cheering and celebrating as well.

--

Do they make themselves known to us? Are there certain ways that we can look for them?

--

Yes, of course.

They are in different dimensions and unless your consciousness is able to travel or meet the frequencies of those dimensions, communication with them may be challenging or require practice.

There are very few humans that have the ability to communicate directly with these beings of light from other dimensions. Direct [telepathic] communication requires that you step up your frequencies and they step down theirs.

They are with you as guides. They come and go. If you want to know when they are there, you may simply ask them to show you signs. Although their signs may not appear in a three-dimensional reality.

--

Can you tell us what the signs from our guides would be like or feel like?

--

You may see, with your open eyes, a sign: which could be a dolphin coming out of the water or a feather blowing in the wind.

But it's more likely that you will feel the vibration of your heart center shift into that which is higher. Or you may feel tingles or chills throughout your body. Or you may see a symbol in your mind, or you may receive a thought form that you will know did not originate from your own mind.

It will vary from person to person, and moment to moment, but the signs are subtle for all.

You may also visit with them in your dream state or in meditation.

--

How is it that the war factions, war machines, military powers, and all that drive this masculine energy of war – how will they allow in the feminine and give up the weapons and the power?

--

Awareness of compassion is rising within all human beings. Also, the young adults and children, who are born with a higher awareness, have spent their lives knowing that fighting is wrong and that it does not resolve anything. So, as they become your leaders, they will make different choices. This is already happening. It will be even more so in the next ten years.

The old energies of war and domination and greed and violence are diminishing as the light on the planet is increasing.

It takes time. It has been over many decades that this shift has slowly been taking place. But you are getting there. This has been a collective choice that humans have made – to work towards world peace and unity and less division, fewer borders. To step into a new Earth, where there is cooperation, compassion, kindness, and a true love for other beings – regardless of your perceived differences.

This is the energy of the divine feminine. It's the energy of compassionate action. Taking action based in the love within your hearts; taking action to make things better for all.

--

What is the responsibility of the individual when met with ideas that are war-like or violent?

--

You encounter this daily. You encounter conflict, you encounter selfishness or greed or blame. And your only responsibility is to step back from the situation, go into your heart center, find your compassionate center, and respond from there. Instead of allowing your ego to react with the mind.

Compassion, empathy, kindness, understanding — these are all manifestations of the divine feminine that is within all human beings, regardless of gender.

Your role is to respond with compassion.

--

7

DIVINE BALANCE

REFLECTION

Farnaz:

For thousands of years, the winter solstice has been celebrated around the planet. Marking the shortest day and longest night of the year, it has long been a grand celebration of the rising sun. From the festival of Saturnalia in ancient Rome to the Fiesta del Sol in ancient Peru, the cycles of nature and rebirth of the light continue to be honored in ceremonies.

On this winter solstice, I am on the island of Maui in Hawaii – the sacred land of the ancient Lemurians, our ancestors. Being on this land and connecting to its energies brought forth visions of these ancient people and the ways in which they honored one another and the cycles of nature.

In my mind's eye, I see men and women gathered in ceremony, singing and gazing lovingly into one another's eyes. As they connect in this way, they acknowledge the innate gifts they each bring to their community and the balancing of masculine and feminine energies.

The men are honored for their connection to the Earth – building shelter, providing food. The women are honored for their connection to the stars – birthing and raising future generations with love and compassion and leading through their innate wisdom and enhanced intuition.

On this winter solstice, I watch the sun rise on this sacred island. The sun presents a portal, through which I travel from the darkness into the light. I leave stagnation behind as I move into a bright, new beginning. The sun gives me a glimpse of a future for humanity, in which we return to the balance of masculine and feminine energies – where we honor the innate gifts we came into this lifetime to share with one another, with the planet, and with the stars.

8

―――――――

THE HEART KNOWS THE WAY
INTRODUCTION

Farnaz:

For the past year or so these channeled messages were only coming through when Kristin and I set the intention, came together, and melded our frequencies to receive them. We would set up our recording device, complete the session, and I would transcribe the messages afterwards. This process had evolved naturally, and we were both quite comfortable with it.

On the day leading to the next message, I was taking my morning walk along the beach, when I intuitively felt the presence of the leopards all around me. I was seeing them in my mind's eye, feeling their strength, and had a knowing that they wanted to communicate further. There was a sense of urgency in their energy.

I returned home from my walk, rolled out my yoga mat in the sun to stretch for a bit, clear my head of the cats, and focus on the imminent workday to begin. The moment I sat down, a voice in my head directed, "Get your journal, you have to write right now." I went inside and grabbed my journal and came back out to my sunny mat. Intuitively, I knew what was happening, even if it was the first time it happened this way. I sat back down, took a few deep breaths, put pen to paper and began channeling – but this time in written rather than spoken words.

What came through, first as thought forms and then as written statements, was from the collective consciousness of the leopards. They posed deep questions for reflection and offered their compassionate observations. Their message focused on the wisdom of the human heart.

9
___

THE HEART KNOWS THE WAY
CHANNELED MESSAGE: LEOPARDS

--

What is your heart's desire?

--

What is standing in your way?

--

Your heart always knows the way but are you listening?

--

You humans waste precious time in thoughts of things that may or may not be or occur in the future. We, in the animal kingdom, do not live this way.

We act on instinct, or what you would call intuition. We are connected to our Divine Source energy 100% of the time. We do not go in and out of this connection with Source as you do.

We do not live in your duality. We live in Oneness.

Humans think that they understand animals, but your understanding of the workings of your world are limited by your conditioning and perceptions.

We are here to share with you that we see ourselves as a thread in the tapestry of creation on this Earth and beyond. We are part of the whole.

You see yourselves as separate. This is an illusion. You, too, are a thread. Your awareness is only one thread. We showed you the vision of the string of beads [in a previous channeling].

You are not capable of seeing the whole with your limited minds. The only way to experience the truth is by feeling into it with your open hearts. You must practice this.

Every moment that you are disconnected from the truth within your heart is an opportunity for doubt, fear, and illusion to enter. It is your conscious choice in every moment to either align with the divine truth or the falsehoods and illusions created by the mind.

This is not an easy practice for the human being.

We are sharing this message with unconditional love and without judgment. We are sharing, so that you have the awareness to commit to this practice of feeling into the truth with the heart, when your mind and ego want to take the reins.

It is your choice. We suggest that you accept that it is a choice. You are not victims of anything other than perhaps the confines and falsehoods of your own minds.

We are here to share with you that there is a gentler, more benevolent way to be in this world. We hope that you find inspiration in the ways of animals in the wild. Everything that they do has a benevolent purpose.

There is no greed, shame, guilt, or waste. Even when one wild animal kills another, it is to feed herself and her young. It is with purpose and with gratitude. Continue your journey with clear purpose and incessant gratitude.

Be aware of your thoughts and emotions. Ensure that they are coming from a place of unconditional love and compassion towards yourself, other human beings, and all sentient life on your planet and beyond.

Thank you for listening to our message.

--

10

THE HEART KNOWS THE WAY
REFLECTION

Farnaz:

Empathy. It is the gift of the human heart.

We are born with an innate ability to perceive experiences from multiple points of view. Yet, we are conditioned to close ourselves off and shut down "the other."

We are disillusioned by the idea of separation to the point that we struggle to live in unity with our fellow humans, not to mention animals, plants, all life on the planet, and the Earth. She is a magnificent living being. We co-create with her. She sustains us and gives so much.

Yet, we have been so disconnected to our innate empathy that we cannot see the big picture. It is as if our conditioning has manifested as a switch that we unconsciously turn on and off.

When on – we feel into experiences with our hearts wide open. We allow ourselves to merge our emotions with those of others. We feel into their joy and into their pain. This awareness brings tears of compassion into our eyes. But we have been conditioned not to live this way.

When off – we go about our experiences with our hearts closed and detached from our emotions. We allow our minds to lead the way, finding some sort of reasoning for the whys and why-nots. We judge situations based on our limited understanding and without compassion. This way of being has not worked out so well for us – collectively – for tens of thousands of years, if not longer.

We read in our history books of barbaric, heartless interactions among groups of people. We observe in today's leadership around the world an abundance of corruption, manipulation, greed, and a general lack of integrity and compassion for all life – humans, animals, and the planet.

Where is the empathy of the human heart, we ask?

It is there – buried deep beneath the falsehoods of our human conditioning, rooted in the fears of survival created by the human mind over millennia.

Our hearts always know the way to compassion, expansion, and unconditional love.

Isn't it time we live from this space?

Where do we begin?

When concepts feel too complex for my limited mind, I tune into my empathic heart. I tend to the small things. I plant seeds.

My mind wants to give up; it tells me I am too small to make a difference.

But my heart knows the way.

Deep down within me, there is a knowing that I am part of the whole and every small action I take with pure intention from my heart will ripple out infinitely.

Empathy and compassion – they are the innate gifts of the human heart. We must cherish these gifts, acknowledge them, and bow down to our own divinity.

We are part of the whole, and the whole is part of us.

11

THE WILD ONES

INTRODUCTION

F arnaz:

In the subsequent weeks, my comfort level with constant communication with these energies from the wild steadied. I would receive glimpses of wisdom here and there, at the most unexpected times. The following message came through in the middle of the night.

I suddenly awoke and looked at the time – 3:33 am. I feel deeply connected to the energies of numbers and these repeating ones, to me, represent divine presence or communication: a sense that the spirit world demands my attention. The number three represents a catalytic energy – one that stirs up existing energies to transmute them into something new.

I sighed and picked up the journal and pen from my bedside table. Without turning on the light, I witnessed my hand automatically moving across the pages as words flowed out. I was half asleep, half awake, and not entirely aware of what was happening. It was not until the next morning, when I unscrambled the written words, that I realized the power of the messages that had come through.

12

THE WILD ONES
CHANNELED MESSAGE: LEOPARDS

--

We are the wild ones.

Untamed. Unconditioned. Unfiltered.

We know who we are.

We aspire to show you who you are so that you may remember, embody it, and teach it to others.

We are a collective consciousness.

We are connected to the All, as you are.

We are both part of the Earth and part of the cosmos, as you are.

We have much in common in the grand scheme of things.

We are here to serve as you are.

We are fierce, yet we are gentle.

Journey with us and you may learn something unexpected.

--

13

THE WILD ONES

REFLECTION

Farnaz:

Wild women, beware.

We have endured so much conditioning since we were young girls.

To speak softly. To think before acting. To walk a certain way. To sit a certain way. To dress appropriately. To watch our boundaries. To be careful. To be patient. To remain poised. To watch our words.

It does not make a difference where on this planet we grew up. The rules we lived by were not the same as those imposed on our brothers.

We innately always knew that something was off. But it was all around us, so we accepted the way things were as the way they were supposed to be.

So here we are.

The wild and free souls that we once were, now tied in knots that are ready to unravel and let loose.

We know who we are at the core. We do not fit into this box that they stuffed us into.

We are strong women – our hearts pounding wildly in our chests – ready to take on the next adventure in this journey called life.

We are ready.

We have been waiting for this moment to scream out to the world in pure love and acceptance for ourselves.

I am a wild woman; and I am free to be me.

14

MINDFULNESS

INTRODUCTION

Farnaz:

A few months passed since our last channeled session with the leopard energies. As a numerology enthusiast, I suggested to Kristin that we should resume our sessions on May 5, 2021 – 555 [5 + 5 + (2+0+2+1)]. These special dates with repeating numbers are considered sacred portals into other dimensions of consciousness.

On this portal day, I began the session with an invocation: "In the frequency of Creative Source energy – in this time, space, and beyond – we open our hearts and our beingness to the transcription of love. We open ourselves up to all natural frequencies through our physical reality now and set the intention for the information we receive and share to be unaltered love and unaltered truth from Source energy only. So be it. So it is."

Although the session began with the wisdom of the leopards, there were other energies present and communicating throughout and they are noted as such.

15

MINDFULNESS

CHANNELED MESSAGE: LEOPARDS & NATURE'S SPIRITS

--

I see a field of clovers.

--

Isn't it a magnificent sight?

--

It is.

--

We must all work together to protect the beauty of the planet.

This will be the main message of this channel.

As we have said before, you experience duality, as human beings. It is your nature to go back and forth between moments of connection to the All and disconnection. Sometimes, you are even disconnected from your own Source energy.

This is the nature of the human being. But this is not the nature of the wild ones. We are connected to Source 100% of the time.

We hope that we can teach you to be more mindful and aware of when you are disconnected, so that you can bring your awareness back into the reconnection.

Without a sense of connection, it will be difficult for us to all work together energetically to protect the sacred life on this planet – from minerals to plants to animals to human beings and beyond.

--

I hear bells clanging.

--

We have shown this before. But this time, we are not speaking of a celebration.

This vision has more to do with the sound frequencies and how they affect all beings on the planet.

We ask you to be more mindful of the sounds that you produce in your modern lifestyles. As these sounds affect plants and animals and their well-being, as well as yours.

There is nothing wrong with the fact that you have busy cities, full of cars and factories and other industrial developments. But as your technologies move towards renewable resources, you will find that the sounds that you produce will change and diminish. The natural and manmade environments will work together more harmoniously than has been in the recent past.

An example that we share is the electric car. If you compare it to you have been used to for the last hundred years, they produce almost no sound while in use.

Does this example make sense?

--

Yes, perfectly.

I see two crescent moons that are back-to-back.

--

Farnaz:

Now some kind of nature's spirit is coming in. I can't put a form to it, but I feel its energy. The leopard is gone.

This spirit is here to speak about the effects of our actions and way of life on realms outside of the Earth plane.

The back-to-back crescents represent the moon: a symbol of realms outside of the planet, or the unseen.

--

I see a big eye and it is pulsating.

--

This eye represents several things.

First, this eye represents the all-knowing and all-seeing aspect of all beings, as they are connected to the Oneness.

It represents the deep awareness you all have intuitively and the knowing that all are one and all are related and working together.

Second, this eye represents your third eye as a reminder. Before you act [on a thought], pause for a moment and ask yourself if your action is potentially harmful to the planet other sentient beings. And if it is, then stop and choose a different action.

Be mindful.

There are major environmental issues that you, as individuals, may feel you cannot do anything about since you are not an environmental activist, a government official, or someone who has the ability to change laws. Just because you feel that you cannot make changes at that massive scale, it does not mean that you are helpless.

If every single human being – truthfully only a small percentage of you – starts to pay attention at the footprint they leave on this planet, everything will shift in the right direction. This is already happening but there is so much more that each individual can do. This shift starts by just being aware and mindful of the footprint that you leave behind.

Your society is full of consumerism. We do not say this to judge as we understand that this is part of modern life. But every day, you may ask yourself, "What can I do today to only use what I need to reduce waste?"

Be mindful of these small actions that you take.

--

I see a group of baby leopards being playful together.

--

Farnaz:

The leopards are back. Nature's spirits are gone.

--

We are asking you to live in joy and be playful.

Without joy, each life is wasted. You are here, in this lifetime, to experience joy and to play. To not be so serious. To be mindful, but not serious. And not to lose your child-like wonder. To move forward in life with all of your senses open to receive each experience. This is the joy of being human and many [humans] miss it.

Due to your conditioning, you may feel that it is irresponsible to be child-like. We are not asking you to relinquish your responsibilities. We are suggesting that every responsibility may still be handled in a joyful and playful way.

This is what the word "enjoy" means. So, we are asking you to enjoy your lives. To live your lives in joy, even in the way that you handle your daily responsibilities – do them in joy.

Regarding your children, remember not to impose so much structure and pressure. They are only children. Do not condition them as you were conditioned. Allow them to live in joy at every age and stage, in a way that is appropriate for them.

You are not here, as parents, to control them. You are only here, as guardians, to keep them safe and on path. Sometimes, you may feel that you are keeping them safe by imposing your own rigid boundaries and expectations on them. We ask you to be mindful of this, too.

Ask yourself, "How much of this is my own conditioning? How much of this is what I think society expects of me as a parent and for my child?"

Then ask yourself, "What feels right in my heart? Is this action necessary? Is it kind or is it hurtful and limiting?"

We, the wild ones, have a completely different approach to raising our young. We follow the laws of the universe. We follow the laws of the planet. We are clear on what our roles are. It is all intuitive for us, there is no conditioning.

It is time for you all to shed your conditioning, one layer at a time. Because your conditioning is getting in the way of your soul evolution and the evolution of humanity as a whole. Humanity's disconnection to your intuition and Source energy is causing harm to other aspects of the planet.

--

I am seeing the ocean at sunset.

--

And isn't that a beautiful sight?

--

Yes.

--

The planet has so much beauty to offer. The spirits of the waters are working hard to keep the oceans clean and to support the life and the life cycles within the oceans. These oceans are what make your planet, or our planet, so special.

Have gratitude for these nature's spirits and for the planet itself. And for all of the energies that are constantly working in unison to keep things moving in the right direction – to heal the waters, to heal the planet. So that the oceans can, in turn, heal you.

You all have experienced the healing that occurs when you place your feet in the sand or take a swim in the ocean or sit in a boat on a lake. Intuitively, you all know the healing power of water and use water to purify and cleanse.

We ask you to remember this vision of the beautiful sunset over the ocean when you take actions that could potentially harm these pristine and beautiful parts of your planet.

--

I see a lemon.

--

We would like to say that the least harmful way to leave a footprint, as a human being, is to only consume what is ready to be consumed for food.

If you look at a lemon – your science shows all of the health benefits, so we do not need to go into it –

there comes a time in its life cycle when it will fall off of the tree, whether your pick it or not.

Your plants are gifting themselves to you. They want you to take them and use them in any way that bene-fits you – whether it's to eat or juice or use for oils, or whatever it is that you need.

We ask you to be mindful and grateful for these gifts that the planet offers you.

We ask you to understand that while we are here to support you, we expect you to respond responsibly in return. Take only what you need and be grateful.

--

I just want to say that I am grateful for these lessons. Thank you for coming to us.

--

You are welcome.

We want you to share these notes. This is why we are here.

--

We will do that.

Is there any other advice on how to share this information beyond publishing it in a book?

--

We believe you have heard this before. You must be a living example. This is the best way to share any information.

Remember that everything you do as an individual has a ripple effect. The frequencies that you put out through the kindness and mindfulness of your actions, send an infinite wave of this frequency outward for others to receive. So even if others are not around you and they do not observe your actions, they will still feel the energies of your actions.

--

Thank you for the reminder.

I see a beautiful, scarlet-colored Ibis.

--

This message is to look to nature as your teacher.

Observe the birds. Take time to observe the birds. Watch how in-tune they are with one another and how gracefully they move.

We ask you to look to nature and observe, so that you can be reminded of how the wild ones commune with nature. They do not feel that they are separated from nature, they understand that they are all one.

Every time you see a bird, or any other creature, just observe in gratitude. And thank them for being your teachers.

--

16

MINDFULNESS

REFLECTION

F arnaz:

All life on the planet is exploring the experience of its own creation.

As human beings, some of our creations, or actions, have disregarded or even devastated the trajectories of other life forms on the planet.

We have not been respectful or responsible. We have not been supportive of other life forms, or the environments necessary for them to survive – let alone thrive.

We were all born with an innate compassion for all life, not just our own. Somewhere along the way, we allowed our conditioning to dismiss this inner knowing that all life is sacred.

It is our long-forgotten responsibility to respond to all life with equivalent respect and reverence. There is no hierarchy to creation. At the core of all life is pure awareness.

We must pause to reconnect to all that is.

We must remember the gifts our souls brought into this lifetime and use them to respond to all life from the expansive heart-soul level, rather than from the limited mind-ego one.

As we begin to live collectively from this place of heart-soul awareness, we may truly be of service to the experiences of all life on the planet – not just our own.

May we, as human beings, respond to all life with responsibility, respect, and reverence.

May all beings be free to explore the experiences of their creations in harmony with one another, and with the planet.

So be it.

17

RECONNECTION

INTRODUCTION

Farnaz:

The day after the last session, Kristin and I came together again to receive more information.

We pulled in and all around us a dome of pastel-colored energies to keep our frequencies steady and our bodies and minds comfortable, so that our spirits would be able to merge with the oneness and channel purely and concisely.

We took the time to connect to Earth and cosmic energies, solar and lunar energies, and sound, light, and love energies – asking them to balance us in divine perfection. We then asked the wild ones to bring forth their authentic wisdom and remained open to receive in gratitude and honor.

After a few moments, I felt a portal slowly pulsating – opening and closing – asking me to go in. I took a few deep breaths and asked Kristin to assist me energetically.

Once in, I felt as though I was traveling into the inner Earth plane. I shared this with Kristin and she asked me to describe my experience.

I shared the following with Kristin.

"I'm still traveling. I haven't really arrived anywhere. I was feeling a bit of tension and part of me was resisting, so I just took a deep breath and let it go. I'm still moving. It feels like it's going to take a while to get there. It feels like a long journey to the inner Earth. But I don't see anything yet.

It seems that I have arrived, at least to the energies that want to communicate. I don't see anything at all, but I feel that I have arrived. Right now, I feel like my heart center is activated and the energies are moving from the back of my heart chakra, pulsating to the front toward you. This is how I usually feel when I'm ready to channel.

This is a collective energy and they are Gaia messengers, or Gaia collective. They reside on the inner Earth plane, a dimension we don't have access to. It's a fifth or sixth dimensional frequency, so it is not 3D at all. They are saying that they belong in the category of nature's spirits – if we want to put them in a box. They are showing me something similar to a classroom setting and basically telling me that I am here to be a student and to learn something from them.

They are asking me to come to this place often. This isn't going to be the only time that they teach. They are saying that it will be an eclectic mix of messages and they want you to ask questions. They want you to ask specific questions related to Earth energies."

18

RECONNECTION

CHANNELED MESSAGE: EARTH SPIRITS

--

*How can humans access Earth energies or connect more with
them?*

--

The most essential way to connect with any type of
Earth energies is through the practice of grounding.

The main way to ground your energy is through
your attention and intention; it helps if you also use
your physical body.

But, for example, if you are somewhere – like on an
airplane – where you cannot [connect to the Earth
with your physical body], you will want to set the
intention to connect energetically to the ground
beneath you. If you are able to connect physically,

place your feet on the floor or sit on the floor. If you are outside, in nature, this is even better [or a stronger connection].

The idea is to allow your consciousness to move from your upper energy centers [downward towards the lower energy centers]. Beginning at the crown of your head or beyond, depending on how far your awareness reaches, pull those higher frequency energies down slowly through your body via your central meridians or spinal column. Slowly allow those energies to flow down, down, down all the way to your feet. And then – ask for all the divine help that you may need – to push the energies from your feet all the way down to the center of the Earth.

Stay in allowance mode. Allow this energetic connection and movement – which some will feel, and some will not, depending on practice – through your body, from the center of the galaxy to the center of the Earth.

This is the practice of grounding.

You set the intention that you will connect to the Earth energies. Then you stay in allowance mode for those energies to move through you as needed. The movement of the energy will feel different every time. You may do this many times throughout your day, as you remember to do it.

Once you set the intention and allow for the movement of this energy to ground you, the energy reaches the center of the Earth. Then, it slowly moves back up into your feet and through the rest of your body, out of your crown and back out to the center of the galaxy.

In this energy exchange – which is how we will refer to the grounding practice – you are acknowledging your place in the universe as a being of both the Earth and the stars. You are supported in both directions by many beings and energies whose are committed to supporting this lifetime of yours.

The Earth sends energy up and the stars send energy down [into your body]. When all of these frequencies are balanced, your awareness will reside in your heart center [chakra]. This is where these energies come together in perfect balance and harmony. This is the space that we want you to be living from at all times – with this balanced energy in your heart center.

--

Thank you.

--

You are welcome.

We will say a few more things about grounding because it is very important.

Grounding is the most critical energetic practice for any human being.

You must remember that plants are grounded at all times. When their roots are pulled out of the soil, they lose their life and vitality. They must be connected to the Earth at all times.

Animals are grounded; even birds in the sky are grounded. Their energy exchange with the Earth is constant and uninterrupted, even if they do not have their feet on the ground.

It is the intention that matters. So, in the case of human beings, your lifestyles have changed so much. You are not walking barefoot on the Earth any longer. The indigenous people and a few other groups are [walking barefoot] but generally, your lifestyles have shifted so much that we are asking you to pay attention to this concept.

You could be walking in nature; you do not have to be barefoot. But being barefoot helps to remove that physical layer of resistance [so that the energy flows more easily].

Walk barefoot, or just walk – in the sand, in the snow, in the grass. You see children love to do this. They do not like to wear shoes or socks. They want to be connected.

This is your human nature – wanting to be connected to the Earth. The electromagnetic fields, or what we are calling energies, or frequencies, are moving back and forth. This energy exchange is essential to your health and vitality as a human being.

This is the practice of grounding.

--

Thank you.

There is beauty when you speak of the connection of plants and animals to the Earth and how they are not separated from the Oneness. Can you expand upon that a bit?

--

The consciousness of different beings varies.

Your awareness as a human being has much broader potential than the awareness of plants and animals in the wild.

Your duality exists to offer you free choice. Without duality there would not be free choice. So, there is a purpose for the duality – it is not positive or negative or good or bad. The wild ones do not have this free choice.

The duality must exist in order for the soul to choose the types of experiences it wants to have. It is through experiences that you choose and learn different lessons in each lifetime. Once you learn the lesson, you carry it with you at the Soul level across all lifetimes.

These lifetimes are not linear, as in occurring one after the next. Even if this is how you sometimes talk about it. You may refer to it as a past life, but really, there is no time.

Time is a construct of your three-dimensional reality and linear time is necessary in the lives you live on Earth. But outside of this frequency of this particular lifetime on this planet, there is no linear time.

Everything is happening in the present moment. So, in this present moment – at a Soul level – you are experiencing many different realities, all of which affect one another. The lessons that you learn in each lifetime are affecting one another as well.

All of these experiences from each lifetime are recorded and stored by the same Soul, or Oversoul. And your Higher Self is the bridge between your awareness in this lifetime and that grander Soul. The purpose of the duality is to give you free choice.

--

How does the free choice of the human being affect the larger universe? What is the purpose of free choice?

--

Consider this planet as one that provides an opportunity for any and all Souls to come here and learn; it is a university. It is an opportunity and an honor to experience a human lifetime on this beautiful planet. This is a special place that offers this free choice.

--

When you talked about Earth being a type of university for Souls to choose, is there a collective lesson that is supposed to be learned and added to the universe's energy?

--

The final lesson for all Souls is reaching a state of enlightenment. Once that level of consciousness has been reached, there is no need to have a physical body or learn any more lessons. The learning is complete at that point. Essentially, enlightenment is a reaching a state of Oneness.

If you look at the scale of consciousness – which is an energetic scale – the lowest frequencies are at the bottom and the highest frequencies are at the top. At the very top is Oneness. At the very bottom is complete separation. Many of you fluctuate somewhere in the middle of this scale. There is a pendulum that swings from Oneness to complete separation – this is the human experience.

When you experience extreme separation, you feel emotions like shame, guilt, or fear – things of that sort. When you experience the higher frequencies, you feel understanding, acceptance, or compassion.

Emotions are your guidance system, so that you can check in [with yourself] and see where you are in that moment. If you recognize that emotions are purely there to guide you, you can allow them to move easily through you rather than identifying with them as who you are.

Allow the emotions to be and to pass, without judgment, instead of over-identifying with each one. The emotions are not who you are; you are a divine Soul. But to be in a human body is to have thoughts and to have emotions. Through the experiences of your guidance system, you learn your lessons.

There are many lessons, not just one. Generally, each Soul is here in each lifetime to learn one major lesson. There may be sub-lessons. But for most of you, there is one greater lesson that you are here to experience and learn for your Soul's evolution. And what you learn in this lifetime affects all parallel lifetimes that your Oversoul is participating in and experiencing.

We showed this concept before as the string of beads in an earlier transmission.

--

For people who are on the path toward enlightenment and work to practice the types of things you have talked about — grounding, living with truth and love in their heart, surrounded by nature — when confronted by others of lower energies such as jealousy or bullying, what is a recommended response to manage these situations?

--

The first is to respond with understanding.

What understanding means in this context is to put judgment aside. But what you all tend to do is say, "Well, I wouldn't do that to someone." Or, "I wouldn't do that to someone. I would do it differently." This is judgment.

So first, remove all judgment and respond with understanding. Say, "Okay, this person has something going on right now that I don't know anything about, and this is the best they can do in this moment." They may be hurting and there is probably something going on that you don't know. If you acknowledge this, then it is possible to respond with understanding.

Once you move past this first step of understanding and non-judgment, the second step is to respond with compassion or take compassionate action.

You may ask, "What can I do to help this situation right now?" And sometimes the answer may be to not respond at all, or to walk away. But sometimes the answer may be to lend a hand, to reach out, or to see if there is any way that you can help this person.

The third step is to respond with love – which can be expressed in many ways. It could be as simple as a genuine smile, or a gentle squeeze of the shoulder, or a hug. Or it could be non-physical, just sending energetic ripples of love from your heart out towards the person. Some people pray silently. Some people ask their angels and guides to help. There are many ways to respond with love.

What we are asking you to do in those challenging or difficult moments is to take a deep and cleansing breath to bring in pure life force energy and give yourself a moment to think and feel before you respond. And then to respond with non-judgement, understanding, compassion, and love.

This is a practice; you will not get it perfect every time. But this is the solution to every problem.

--

19

RECONNECTION

REFLECTION

Kristin:

This message is basically a Cliff's Notes version of how to live a happy and connected life.

I could design an awesome weeklong retreat around the simple, yet profound, messages in this ten-page channeling from the Earth spirits. I encourage you to read this section multiple times, soak in the advice, and put it into practice.

Right now, I am most enjoying the idea of "emotions as a guidance system." It is so easy for me to grab onto my emotions and believe that they are who I am… my defining force.

I am so happy…

Look at that great big, beautiful ocean that exists just for me...

I am one lucky Mama...

And later that day, *I am so hurt...*

People can be so unfair and unkind...

Why is this world filled with so much pain?

In our first book, I wrote about my ability to live presently, which can be quite delightful when life is going well, but when I'm down it can feel like I'm drowning. The advice to use emotions as a guidance system – to let emotions be and to pass, without judgment, instead of over-identifying with each one, is helpful.

I am more than my emotions; I am more than my emotions... I feel a mantra coming on.

And can we pause for a moment to recognize that this channeling has given us "a solution for every problem." I'm just going to say, "thank you" and reread that section again and again until it seeps into my heart and brain and becomes second nature to me.

20

SPIRAL OF CONSCIOUSNESS
INTRODUCTION

Farnaz:

For the past several years, as my spiritual journey has deepened, I have become aware of the existence of other dimensions, or many versions of reality. As human beings on Earth, we collectively live in a three-dimensional world. However, as our collective consciousness expands, we begin to experience the fourth and fifth dimensions – and beyond.

There are times when we understand something or can mentally process the information – this is knowledge, directed by the mind. Then, there are times that we possess an innate knowing, without understanding at all – this is wisdom, directed by the heart.

As we expand in consciousness, we meld the knowledge of the mind with the wisdom of the heart – we become whole, limitless, and accepting of our multi-dimensional nature. The following channel, that came through as I was journaling after meditation, describes the human journey of evolution.

21

SPIRAL OF CONSCIOUSNESS
CHANNELED MESSAGE: LEOPARDS

\-\-

Hello to our dear human beings.

We are delighted to communicate with you in this manner. We smile with pleasure in this reconnection of human consciousness and wild animal consciousness. We merge our awareness into one another's.

As we have said before we are all part of the tapestry of creation. We are part of the Oneness and we ARE the Oneness.

There is no beginning and no end to our awareness. We are infinite in all directions.

\-\-

Today we wish to speak about the rising of consciousness.

We will use the terms low and high, not to place emphasis or rank – that is what the linear mind of the human being does – but to refer to them energetically.

Denser, lower vibrations exist in the three-dimensional realm, or your physical reality. Lighter, higher vibrations exist in the fourth and fifth dimension, or the spiritual realm.

Again, your linear minds lean towards categorization and may immediately organize these dimensions as 3, 4, and 5, one after the other. This is not the way the universe works.

There are no straight lines [in the universe] – beginnings or endings. Everything [in the universe] is part of a spiral, or fractal. All is infinite in all directions – up and down, side to side.

Visualize a circle in two dimensions. Now visualize the circle in three dimensions and it becomes a sphere. This sphere can contract and expand infinitely.

There are no limitations in sacred geometry [or shapes that exist in nature].

--

Now, let us speak of the spiral of consciousness.

As the human consciousness expands, it moves from the lower vibrations to the higher ones. This is a universal law in that it is true in all of creation's matrices.

Imagine a coiled spiral that moves up and down infinitely in all directions. Imagine your level of consciousness moving about this spiral from lower to higher levels.

The lower levels of the spiral represent the survival-type instincts where humanity has been for tens of thousands of years – as recorded in your history books [focused on wars, famine, lack].

You [humans] are moving into the new Golden Age [of planet Earth] and your consciousness is expanding – moving from lower to higher levels.

With increased awareness, or an expanded consciousness, you move away from surviving and into thriving.

Thriving means that you use your three-dimensional [earthly] experiences as opportunities to create, grow, learn, and reflect.

With each experience that you master, you become aware of other points-of-view. You take this expanded awareness with you as you move forward into your next experience, in the form of a new perspective. You repeat this cycle of experience again and again.

The spiral of consciousness is a metaphor that we share to assist you in visualizing the effects of experiences on the expansion of your consciousness.

--

Enjoy the ride. We will be here to support you in all of the ways that we do.

Thank you for listening to our wisdom.

--

22

SPIRAL OF CONSCIOUSNESS

REFLECTION

Farnaz:

I sit on the beach with my feet in the sand as a gentle breeze moves across my face. As I look around, witnessing the small shells scattered about, I reflect on one of the most ancient creatures of the Earth: the nautilus.

A symbol of nature's grace, the nautilus represents growth, expansion, and renewal. I recall from my days of studying architecture the concept of the Golden Section, in art the concept of Divine Proportion, and in mathematics the Fibonacci sequence — all describing the spiral logarithms occurring in nature.

The nautilus is one of thousands of nature's wonders to reveal itself as a spiral. Order amongst chaos. Precision.

I am reminded of my own continuous journey of discovery, learning, and growth; of recycling previous points-of-view; experiencing my reality through a different lens; and beginning once again.

Spiritual evolution.

23

FLOW

INTRODUCTION

Farnaz:

A pilgrimage.

The pilgrimage is a journey with intention: going into unfamiliar territory as a means of discovery and exploration.

This is a metaphor for allowing our consciousness to wander from one state to another.

I'm walking along the coast and even though I have been here before, this time feels different – because I set the intention to come here to be alone and receive divine wisdom.

I brought my journal, thinking that I may channel messages and write them down, but now I see that I don't have a pen in my bag. This moment is fleeting, and I will not remember the information coming into my consciousness. I decide to use my phone recorder and speak out loud versus writing quietly. This is the first time I am channeling in this way, alone and without Kristin. This feels a bit awkward, but I continue to speak into my phone.

As I walk down the bluffs to the water, I feel as though I am on a pilgrimage to a sacred place – to the edge, where the land meets the water.

I am going there to listen to the spirits of the waters to hear what they have to say.

They called me here this morning, asking me to set aside time and sit with them, so that they can share their collective wisdom with me.

I get to the end of my trail, and I find my rock, where I sit and put my things down gently.

I take a few deep breaths and ground my energy down to the center of the Earth, asking her energies to balance my field. I then connect my field to the center of the galaxy, asking for my cosmic frequencies to be balanced.

I pull the Earth and cosmic frequencies together at my heart center, asking for my love frequencies to be balanced. I ask the ocean waves to balance my sound frequencies and bring all these frequencies into divine perfection.

I ask all of nature's spirits to support me. I ask all my guides to support me in being a clear channel for communication with whatever it is that the spirits of the waters want to share with me.

I allow the words to flow out of my mouth, slowly and deliberately and in divine truth.

24

FLOW

CHANNELED MESSAGE: WATER SPIRITS

--

Welcome.

--

We want to speak with you about the state of flow, which is what you experience when you are in divine alignment with your highest calling and your Higher Self.

When you are in this state, time stands still. You feel a sense of openness to what you are experiencing in that moment – childlike wonder, joy, gratitude, peace.

This is the state of flow.

--

When you are in the flow, there is zero resistance.

All is fluid and clear of impurities. These are impurities of thought, feeling, and action.

We, as the spirits of the waters, are here to remind you to live every moment of your life in the flow state.

--

Flow is a way of being, like love is a way of being.

Flow is part of all of creation.

Let water be your reminder to stay in a state of flow, without resistance – with wonder, without agendas or goals – just to experience purely one moment to the next.

Allow the path to be revealed.

--

Many of you feel the state of flow when you are doing things that you love, or you are connecting to people that you love, or when you are communing in nature.

Flow is a stillness, calmness, and an overall sense of wholeness that you feel – like there is nothing missing – and all that you want or need is with you in that moment.

For those of you who are artists, musicians, or doing any type of craft that you enjoy, your creative expression or output takes place in a state of flow.

Flow occurs in those moments where you feel free to purely express your soul's desires – be it cooking, walking, hiking, swimming, or meditation.

Your science shows that the brain waves induced in the state of flow boost your immune system – keeping you young, vital, and full of life.

Your science also shows that extended states of flow reverse the aging process. Your scientists already know this.

We, as the spirits of the waters, are here to remind you that there is no other way that you [humans] were intended to live this life.

--

Be in the flow.

--

25

FLOW

REFLECTION

K ristin:

Is there anything more relaxing than being in a state of flow? When I teach people how to meditate, I talk about relaxing into the alpha brain wave state – the right here/right now state-of-being that isn't concerned with the past or the future. That feels like the beginning of the flow state.

But real-life flow – like when it happens naturally and I'm fully connecting with my kid while doing some fun craft project or with my husband when we're being silly with our cats – feels like the most satisfying, heart-warming state. I want to live in this flow state forever.

I love that the water spirits are here to remind me that the flow state is the way we are intended to live.

It's easy to let the problems of the past and worries of the future make my brain scrambled and mushy, but there is huge value in breathing myself back into a balanced state and just releasing into the flow.

26

SUMMER SOLSTICE
INTRODUCTION

Farnaz:

The summer solstice – marking the midpoint and the longest day of the year – invites us to embrace the sun as we continue our journey from darkness to light. This astrological event is a turning point, as the sun reaches its maximum light and heat, that invokes within us a desire to take action. The sun is represented by the element of fire – providing light and warmth, but more importantly the ability to transmute and transform energies.

On this magical evening, Kristin and I found ourselves in a friend's yard, under an equally magical guava tree. We were accompanied by two friends. The four of us seated in a circle around the trunk of the tree, ready to hear the messages coming through.

I sensed that we were surrounded by a circular energy of light beings, reminiscent of a golden hoop, who were there to encompass us with a celebratory frequency.

We closed our eyes and tuned into this frequency, as I asked all of nature's spirits to connect our energetic roots around the guava tree and through the Earth. I then asked all divine spirits to connect our hearts to one anothers', as well as the center of the tree, like the spokes of a wheel so that we could all communicate in divine truth. After a few minutes of connection, Kristin announced that she felt a moon spirit on her right side. I felt it, too, and so the messages began.

27

SUMMER SOLSTICE

CHANNELED MESSAGE: MOON & FIRE SPIRITS

--

We have just come through a beautiful eclipse. Now we are embarking upon a full moon in a few days, along with the solstice time. Can you tell us if there are any special ceremonies or prayers or meditations that we should do to open ourselves up to the special happenings of this time within the universe?

--

I am here to show my appreciation for your gathering. I am also here to remind you to gather under the moonlight whenever possible, especially in the summer months, when the moon is visible.

I ask that you acknowledge my brilliance in the dark sky. And I ask that you see yourselves as brilliant beings of light, even when you are surrounded by darkness.

I ask you to celebrate the light.

Both in the night sky and anytime there is lightness in nature or in your ways of being.

I ask you to acknowledge and celebrate this light.

I am here to remind you of the nature of the phases that you go through.

I ask you to remember that the experiences that you have are in passing, as are the phases of the moon.

Your task is to stay present in each experience with the knowing that it will pass.

You will always come back to your brilliance of light.

Nighttime is your time to turn inward, to stop doing and just be. Make time every evening to go within in whatever format you choose. Turn off all outside noise and all distractions and focus on the divine wisdom within you before you drift off to sleep. The journey continues while you are sleeping.

This is my message on the longest night of the year: summer solstice.

--

I see a falcon – or a falcon spirit.

--

The falcon is here as spirit guide and guardian for this session. He is watching over us, while enhancing the transmission through my [Farnaz's] third eye.

--

I see three feathers – like crow feathers.

--

The symbol represents a crow or raven's feathers, also spirit guides.

The number three represents a catalyst for transformation.

We are all undergoing transformation and we can ask for the spirit of the raven to come in to assist when we need a boost or extra support in any of kind of spiritual or alchemical work that we are doing.

--

The spirit of the fire behind us, with a masculine energy, speaks. He says this solstice is centered around the burning up and dissolution of all paradigms and energies that no longer serve us. He would like for each one of us to take nine deep breaths, with each breath he will dissolve a layer or aspect that we are ready to release.

--

[Nine slow, deep breaths]

--

28

SUMMER SOLSTICE
REFLECTION

Farnaz:

I love the summer season more than any other, and I have since I can remember. The long, warm days, rich with play, celebrations and gatherings, fill me with laughter and joy. The summer solstice, when the Earth tilts close to the sun, marks the longest day and shortest night of the year.

These rare astrological moments throughout the year hold special meaning for some of us and we create rituals or ceremonies around them. The summer solstice is energetically charged with more light than any other – a moment to turn inward and reflect on the nourishment needed for our continued evolution and growth.

The channeled message from the Moon spirit settles into my heart. She urges us to remember our brilliance of light, even in the darkest of times, and that all phases of our lives are in passing, so we stay present in each moment and experience.

29

I AM THAT

INTRODUCTION

Farnaz:

Crystal Cove – I've been coming here (almost) daily for years. Rarely does a day get missed. I come here to just be and breathe. It's a special spot where I feel fully connected within and without. It is here that I feel the presence of a white horse, one of my spirit guides.

Two summers ago, Kristin and I planned a sound healing session for a small group in this cove. We arrived just after sunrise to set up our instruments. As we walked closer to the shoreline, we unexpectedly found the most magnificent sight: a work of art etched in the still-wet sand. The tide had just lowered, revealing an intricate design of gigantic concentric circles and arcs, stretching over 200 yards – without a footprint in sight.

Kristin and I stared in awe at this work of art, reminiscent of a crop circle, then looked at each other with a knowing that we were not alone on this day. We understood this experience as a communication from a higher dimension and a gift to be received in gratitude.

I come here again today, with gratitude and an open heart, on a quest for inspiration. The moment I place my feet in the warm sand, feel the sun's rays on my skin and the ocean breeze in my hair, pure serenity washes over my entire being. I walk to the water's edge and allow the waves to welcome me to this sacred site. As I breathe in the pure, fresh air, I hear her message unfolding slowly and gently, phrase by phrase.

30

I AM THAT

CHANNELED MESSAGE: AIR SPIRIT

--

Welcome to a new awareness of air – I am that.

I am that which binds all to the one.

I am that which is in everything; and everything is within me.

There is no separation, my child.

I am your mother, as you are mine. Mother and child, child and mother. We are one in the same – united as one.

Each time you inhale, I fill your entire being with life force energy. You infuse it with your essence and exhale it back out into the universe. Every particle of air is infused with the All.

Do you see, my child?

I am in you, through the breath. You are in me, through the breath. Your breath is the only constant, from the wind of birth to the wind of death, from moment to moment and in every transition.

Remember me, for I am that. Air – the only constant.

Breathe me in with gratitude, breathe out to release that which is no longer serving you. I will take it away.

I am that. As you are.

--

31

I AM THAT

REFLECTION

Farnaz:

I step out on my patio for a moment to listen.

I hear the rustle of tree branches gently kissing one another, while the brass wind chimes sing a song praising nature.

The wind blows through my hair and against my skin.

In the distance, I hear the rhythmic hammering of nails, as construction workers continue to build a home down the street.

We are always juggling this duality of being and doing.

Sometimes, I wonder if life is this way in all cultures or if it is this way more so in the so-called developed nations.

We are so hungry to chase our dreams that we forget to pause long enough to take in the beauty of what already surrounds us.

The sight of flowers blooming.

The sound of birds chirping.

The scent of jasmine vines.

The feeling of sunshine on our skin.

The knowing that all is well in this very moment.

I remind myself to breathe into this moment and breathe out the to-dos weighing on my shoulders.

Spiritual wisdom teaches us that this moment is the only reality and linear time is an illusion of the three-dimensional world.

It may take me an entire lifetime of practice to integrate this concept, but I keep at it.

Because it is only in each individual moment that I feel whole, complete, infinite.

I breathe in life force to lift me up; I breathe out all that weighs me down.

32

MAGIC OF DARKNESS
INTRODUCTION

Farnaz:

One evening in late summer, Kristin and I gathered outside with a few close friends to call forth nature's spirits under the stars. We began with intention and meditation, sitting on the ground in a circle, with the moon dimly illuminating our faces.

As I closed my eyes, I saw – with my inner eye – a dark colored jaguar, deep blue, almost black, with spots. She introduced herself as the one who works with the magic of the darkness. She communicated the significance of nighttime and the mysticism it offers. She explained the melding or alchemy of energies that are only possible during the nighttime hours. The jaguar showed me that she had no fear of the unseen or unknown. She signaled for me to follow her lead in this fearlessness.

As my inner sight expanded, the majestic dark cat revealed a bright crystalline spark in her heart center – as confirmation that all living beings of all kingdoms hold this divine spark. She showed me that only through the heart energy we are able connect to beings of all kingdoms – minerals, plants, animals, and other humans.

The jaguar then leapt up – in one swoop – to the branches of a large tree. As she sat in the dark of the night, observing her surroundings, she began to speak to me in images and thought forms, which I did my best to translate into words.

33

MAGIC OF DARKNESS
CHANNELED MESSAGE: JAGUAR

--

Even in the darkness, there can be illumination. You can see even with your eyes closed. You must be able to see with all your senses.

Sometimes the gift of sight is only offered through intuition where the seeing occurs internally, with eyes closed.

Relish the nighttime, even if you are sleeping. Because that is the time that Spirit is working with you – unobstructed, without resistance.

You do not have to be asleep, but you do have to be closed off to outside noise or information.

For this reason, nighttime has always been held sacred for ceremony or inward reflection and introspection.

This is where your power lies, in the observation when all else appears to be dark and invisible. You will be shown the way.

--

34

MAGIC OF DARKNESS

REFLECTION

F arnaz:

A few weeks after the summer solstice, I took a pilgrimage to Sedona to reconnect with the energy of the Red Rocks and recalibrate. While there, I shared the experience of the wild cat channelings with a close friend and mentor, who suggested I meet her friend for a spirit animal reading.

Although I had always believed in animals as spirit guides, I never considered this type of reading session. I had always known that animals carry energies, or attributes, that we can access or tap into to guide different aspects of our lives. With all this leopard and jaguar energy in my consciousness, I decided I was up for the adventure.

I met with Jim, the gifted medicine man, who introduced me to his process, the indigenous teachers, and life experiences that acted as his guides. The details of the session and spirit animal journey Jim guided me through on that day is a book within itself. However, within the many animal energies surrounding me as guides, three of them were wild cats – leopard, lion, and tiger. I was both shocked and serene. I started to laugh nervously and shake my head with disbelief.

All this time that the wild cats were communicating with me, it never occurred to me that they were an aspect of me. It didn't register in my awareness that we are ALL connected as living beings. My ego had stepped in and pushed aside my Higher Self – that part of me that innately knows that the Oneness is the only reality.

I took a deep breath, with a smile on my face – feeling gratitude for the animal spirit guides and for Jim, the gifted medicine man, for reminding me, yet again, that we are all merely threads of one tapestry of creation.

35

AUTUMN EQUINOX

INTRODUCTION

Kristin:

As Farnaz and I were relaxing into the channeling energy on this Autumn Equinox, she was restless. This is not normal for her. She is usually calm and still and focused. But today her body was seeking something different and when she finally got up from her regular position across from me on the floor and moved to the couch to be near Sasquatch, who was sitting in the window, she let out a sigh and was ready to settle into the flow.

--

I feel big jaguar energy.

--

Farnaz:

The jaguars are connecting with me through my heart. They are a mid-night blue color – almost black.

They are circling around the altar that we have set up, while placing all of us in a pyramid structure to protect and contain the energies that we will be co-creating during this session. They want the session to be pure in communication and without interference by other energies.

--

I see a rosy mist around us.

--

The rosy mist is the spirit of the rose quartz at the center of this altar. She asks us to stay in the heart center and to stay in the love frequency – always, but especially during this session. She will anchor the wisdom that comes through into the heart of the planet.

--

36

AUTUMN EQUINOX

CHANNELED MESSAGE: JAGUARS

--

Today is the autumn equinox. It's a beautiful time all over the world, where the days are balanced, and the weather is temperate. Can you tell us, from the perspective of nature, more about what we should know about this time of the year?

--

This time of year marks the moment that the laws of nature and the laws of spirit are in balance. The two work together.

Whether you are aware of it or not, in your lives, you are always working with the natural laws and the spiritual laws. And they must balance one another.

The natural laws are connected to the Earth energies. The spiritual laws are connected to the cosmic energies. They come together at your heart center, and they must be balanced. Too much of one and two little of the other causes suffering in the human being.

This moment, or this date, is a reminder to step back and re-evaluate your lives. Ask your guides to show you what you need to do, or what habits or states of being you need to change, in order to find your own personal balance.

The autumn equinox is a time of reset. It is a time to slow down the activities to balance active and receptive states of being – masculine and feminine energies, day and night, darkness and light. You must allow a certain level of surrender in order to flow with these natural cycles of the planet.

--

I see beautiful golden sun.

--

The autumn equinox is also a time to receive the pure rays of the universe and to give it back. The cosmic light that begins at the center of all that is – at Source energy – originating from the Great Central Sun. This cosmic light then beams into the Galactic Sun, which then beams into the Star Sun of your Milky Way galaxy.

It is a time to receive these cosmic rays into your being through your third eye, and bring them down into your heart center, and into the lower chakras that connect down to the center of the Earth. Thank Mother Earth for receiving and giving back the light that moves through you and back out into the universe – all the way back to the Great Central Sun.

--

Please explain what the Great Central Sun and Galactic Sun are.

--

There are many realms beyond this galaxy and beyond your scientists' awareness.

You are all aware that planet Earth revolves around your Star Sun. Your Star Sun revolves around the Galactic Sun.

Different galaxies and their suns revolve around the Galactic Sun.

The Galactic Sun and all galaxies that revolve around it then revolve around the Great Central Sun – the highest level of Source energy light, or frequency.

This frequency must be stepped down to levels that human beings can receive.

--

Is there a message around children? I see little animal cubs.

--

The awakened parents, who receive direct communication from spirit into their hearts, have a responsibility not only to teach the universal truth to their own children, but also to assist other parents, guardians, caretakers, and teachers in doing the same.

These Star children already know the universal truth, with a capital T. But it is your responsibility to ensure that they do not forget the truth, through the conditioning and falsehoods created over hundreds of thousands of years and the human disconnection with all that is.

Allow your children to spend time in unaltered areas of the natural environment – forests, deserts, mountains, oceans, lakes, rivers – in as much variety as is accessible to you.

Allow them to spend time immersed in the pure energies of the natural environment and the energies of Gaia, away from technology and three-dimensional illusions.

Allow them these experiences often, so that they will remember where they came from, where they are going, what they are here to do, what their purpose is in this lifetime.

Allow them to follow their joys and their passions as they grow into adulthood. It is only from the frequencies of joy and passion that they can take action to fulfill their paths and to experience all that they are here to partake, for their souls to evolve to the next level of consciousness.

As they interconnect daily with Earth's energies and the energies of animals, plants, and minerals, it will be unlikely, even impossible, for them to forget who they are.

This practice is just as important for adults as it is for children. Be mindful in nature, observing with all of the senses – seeing, feeling, touching, and smelling all of the elements around you. When taking a walk in the woods, or watching the sand move in the desert, or swimming with the dolphins in the ocean: observe.

Be grateful and bow down to the energies of Mother Earth and all her inhabitants.

Bow down in gratitude and enjoy the wonder and the beauty that surrounds you.

Prioritize time to step away from your responsibilities: from phones, computers, and buildings that are disconnected from nature.

Allow time to be balanced and healed by the elements – earth, water, fire, and air.

It is critical for you to be in the sun and to allow the light frequencies from the cosmos to balance and harmonize all layers of your being – physical, emotional, mental, and spiritual.

--

Let's discuss the leaders that we, as human beings, have chosen to lead us. Let's focus on the United States and how we may choose differently in the future.

--

The choices you have in leadership right now are not ideal for any of you. They are polarized, which is why it is difficult for many of you to whole-heartedly accept any of them. This transition will take several generations to reconcile.

We spoke of the significance of your roles as awakened teachers to your Star children, who have entered the Earth at a higher vibration that you did. They are less likely to forget where they came from, or their connection to Source energy. They are more likely to lead with compassion – from the heart – than has been done in the past.

These Star children will become the leaders of the future, and by that time, what you now see as leadership will be done with integrity and a focus on what is good for all inhabitants of your planet – human beings, animals, plants, minerals, and the planet itself. This is not the case at this moment.

--

This sounds very hopeful. Can you see our future?

--

We can only see the potentials. You all have free will, so the potentials shift as you all shift in consciousness and action. At this time, you are headed in this direction that we describe.

--

Thank you.

--

We have one more thing to say.

We, as the panther collective consciousness, are here to remind you of the intricate web of creation and the interconnection of all that is.

Never forget balance within yourself.

It is only through the balance within that you may see reflected outwards balance around you. Each human being, as an individual, must be in balance for there to be harmony among all human beings and harmony with all beings and your planet.

This is our message.

--

37

AUTUMN EQUINOX
REFLECTION

Farnaz:

Until my profound experiences of energetic communication with the wild cats, I did not know much about these majestic beings. Although at first glance, leopards and jaguars appear almost the same, I learned that they are quite different. Leopards, *Panthera Pardus*, are native to Africa and Asia while Jaguars, *Panthera Onca*, are native to the Americas.

Jaguars are the largest cats in the Americas and the third largest cats in the world. They are stronger and heavier than leopards, with more powerful jaws. Leopards have more elongated bodies and longer tails, hence move faster than jaguars. The bodies of both wild cats are covered with rosettes, or rose-like markings on their fur, used to camouflage them for defense and stalking prey without being seen. Black panthers are variants of both species. Their dark, almost black coloring and rosettes hide and protect them during nocturnal hunting.

In late fall, I went back to Sedona and met up with Jim, the medicine man. So much had transpired in my journey with the spotted cats since the last time we had met. My questions led to a two-day discussion on jaguar worship among of various indigenous tribes in the Central and South America regions.

I learned about the Matses of the upper Amazon, the pre-Mayan Olmec of Mexico, and the Shuar of Ecuador and Peru. Through ceremony and the use of local plant medicines, the tribespeople connected to the spirit of the jaguar. Once connected, they harnessed the energies of these powerful beings to access the hidden, unseen realms.

To these tribes, jaguars represented nocturnal vision and hunting knowledge, essential to their survival. Thousands of years later, human survival is no longer dependent on hunting for food, but hunting for knowledge. Turning inward is essential to the survival of the human species, as we navigate our own darkness, shadows, and the unknown fate of our futures as beings on this planet.

May we call upon the spirit of the jaguar, to guide us in seeing the hidden duality of nature and the universe. May we all be inspired by the wild cats to tap into the wisdom of the realms hidden within, waiting to be explored.

38

WILD WISDOM

CHANNELED MESSAGE: ELEPHANT

Farnaz:

From a distance, I see a clan of majestic elephants walking towards me across the plains. The sun rises behind them, illuminating their silhouettes with a golden glow.

The elephants represent my ancestors – ancient wisdom coming towards me. They represent a gentle strength, as they step ever-so-lightly on the Earth with their colossal feet.

The leader of the clan, a female, is at the center. As she walks closer to me, she stops and looks at me with her compassionate eyes. She reminds me to listen deeply, as she does with her enormous ears.

She urges me to acknowledge the lessons of the past and present as I move toward the future. She asks me to draw upon my memory of the past, to forgive myself and others, and to tread on the planet with wisdom and compassion.

She reminds me to keep my feet on the ground as I reach for the stars.

AFTERWORD

Kristin:

As we were putting the finishing touches on this book, my 9-month-old kitten, Sasquatch, started acting odd. Over the course of ten days, he went from being a little less active than usual, to experiencing major neurological trauma, including a terrifying, middle-of-the night seizure. After the seizure, and with an animal neurologist helping us along, it became clear that we needed to help him leave his little body. It was the most devastating animal loss I've ever experienced.

He was such a special boy. From the beginning it was clear that he was meant to be in my life. We went through weeks of adoption failures until he popped up, with his weird white undercoat with black tips and all of his 23 toes (domestic cats usually have 18 toes). He walked into our house with supreme confidence and immediately took to our other cat, a floppy rag doll named Milo, who has had every bit of wildness bred out of him.

Sasquatch would sleep on my face every night and follow me everywhere. He was especially interested in being by my side when I was meditating or doing Reiki, and I knew that he could feel the extra energies in the room because of the way he looked at me – super still with his golden eyes wide.

The only person whom he loved as much as my family was Farnaz. They had a bond and always found each other when she visited. If she was in the house, he was in her lap. It was a pure soul connection and it was unmistakable.

I'm not sure why Sasquatch was with us for such a short amount of time and met such a traumatic end, but I do know this: my family's love for that kitten was massive and he lived a beautiful life in Hermosa Beach and he was awed by some amazing big cat energy in my meditation room. So, while we are incredibly sad to be without him, there is some comfort in knowing how very loved he was his whole life and how much fun we had with him while he was with us.

I like to imagine he was reborn a big, confident panther and is running free in the African Savannah, with a lot of extra toes to steady his step. Go and be, wild one.

ABOUT THE AUTHORS

FARNAZ N. RENEKER

A seeker and creator at heart, Farnaz N. Reneker was drawn into the world of visual arts and music as a child. She eventually pursued an education in architecture, where she became engrossed in the study of sacred geometry, the built structures of ancient civilizations, and the art and architecture of the Renaissance.

She began a deep dive into metaphysics in the year 2000 but didn't fully explore its depths until a few years later, when her professional career as an architect led her to Los Angeles. The magic of living near the Pacific Ocean catapulted Farnaz's spiritual journey, which has since evolved into studying the ways of the ancient oracles, priestesses, and healers, while exploring her innate and intuitive gifts.

From channeling divine inspiration through painting and prose to working with individuals or groups, her passion is to facilitate the awakening of the deep wisdom that has always been within all of us.

FARNAZ@THELOVEFREQUENCY.ORG
WWW.THELOVEFREQUENCY.ORG

KRISTIN WHITE

Kristin White spent many years as an event planner and political fundraiser (including a stint at the White House) until the calling came to live her passion: music and meditation. Settling in Hermosa Beach, California to raise her family, she drew upon her musical roots and her meditation practice to co-found White Light Sounds, a sound bath and meditation business.

Kristin incorporates many high vibrational instruments in her sound baths, including gongs, crystal singing bowls, Tibetan singing bowls, Native American flute, chimes, frame drum, shruti box, tongue drum, and vocal toning.

Kristin compliments her sound bath practice as a meditation instructor and retreat and workshop facilitator; and as a Reiki Master, she infuses all of her healing modalities with universal healing energy. Her work as a channeling teacher and facilitator was realized through the process of working with Farnaz on the development of their books.

———

KRISTIN@WHITELIGHTSOUNDS.COM
WWW.WHITELIGHTSOUNDS.COM

———

ALSO BY FARNAZ N. RENEKER & KRISTIN WHITE

[AVAILABLE ON AMAZON, BARNES & NOBLE, APPLE BOOKS, KOBO]